GAPS DIET

MEGA BUNDLE – 2 Manuscripts in 1 – 80+ GAPS - friendly recipes including roast, ice-cream, pie and casseroles for a delicious and tasty diet

TABLE OF CONTENTS

Introduction

GAPS recipes for personal enjoyment but also for family enjoyment. You will love them for sure for how easy it is to prepare them.

ROAST RECIPES

ROASTED SQUASH

Serves: ***3-4***

Prep Time: ***10*** Minutes

Cook Time: ***20*** Minutes

Total Time: ***30*** Minutes

INGREDIENTS

- 2 delicata squashes
- 2 tablespoons olive oil
- 1 tsp curry powder
- 1 tsp salt

DIRECTIONS

1. **Preheat the oven to 400 F**
2. **Cut everything in half lengthwise**
3. **Toss everything with olive oil and place onto a prepared baking sheet**
4. **Roast for 18-20 minutes at 400 F or until golden brown**
5. **When ready remove from the oven and serve**

ROASTED CUCUMBER

Serves: *3-4*

Prep Time: *10* Minutes

Cook Time: *20* Minutes

Total Time: *30* Minutes

INGREDIENTS

- **2 lb. cucumber**
- **2 tablespoons olive oil**
- **1 tsp curry powder**
- **1 tsp salt**

DIRECTIONS

1. **Preheat the oven to 400 F**
2. **Cut everything in half lengthwise**
3. **Toss everything with olive oil and place onto a prepared baking sheet**
4. **Roast for 18-20 minutes at 400 F or until golden brown**
5. **When ready remove from the oven and serve**

ZUCCHINI SOUP

Serves: ***4***

Prep Time: ***10*** Minutes

Cook Time: ***20*** Minutes

Total Time: ***30*** Minutes

INGREDIENTS

- 1 tablespoon olive oil
- 1 lb. zucchini
- ¼ red onion
- ½ cup all-purpose flour
- ¼ tsp salt
- ¼ tsp pepper
- 1 can vegetable broth
- 1 cup heavy cream

DIRECTIONS

1. In a saucepan heat olive oil and sauté zucchini until tender
2. Add remaining ingredients to the saucepan and bring to a boil
3. When all the vegetables are tender transfer to a blender and blend until smooth
4. Pour soup into bowls, garnish with parsley and serve

BEAN SOUP

Serves: *4*

Prep Time: *10* Minutes

Cook Time: *230* Minutes

Total Time: *240* Minutes

INGREDIENTS

- **2 cups beans**
- **1/2 tsp salt**
- **2 cups chicken broth**
- **7 cups water**
- **2 tsp sauce**
- **½ 10-ounce package onions**
- **2 clove garlic**
- **3 bay leaves**
- **½ tsp dried rosemary**
- **1 tsp dried sage**
- **2 tsp dried thyme**

DIRECTIONS

1. **Place the bean mixture in a pot with the rest of ingredients**
2. **Cook over medium heat until the soup boils**
3. **Reduce the heat and simmer for 3-4 hours**

4. **When ready remove from heat and serve**

SIDE DISHES

RICE PAPER ROLLS

Serves: ***4***
Prep Time: ***10*** Minutes

Cook Time: ***15*** Minutes

Total Time: ***25*** Minutes

INGREDIENTS

- **1 cucumber**
- **1 red capsicum**
- **1 carrot**
- **1 avocado**
- **2 oz. pea sprouts**
- **¾ coriander**
- **¾ cup mint**
- **2 oz. peanuts**
- **2 tablespoons chili sauce**
- **1 tablespoon soy sauce**
- **2 tablespoons lime juice**

DIRECTIONS

1. **Place all the vegetables on a plate**
2. **In a bowl mix chili sauce, lime juice and soy sauce**

3. **Some one rice paper roll in a bowl of water and then place vegetables on the wrapper**
4. **Fold up the bottom of the wrapped, and roll u to enclose filling**
5. **Place on a tray, serve with dipping sauce**

CHICKEN NOODLE SALAD

Serves: ***4***

Prep Time: ***10*** Minutes

Cook Time: ***30*** Minutes

Total Time: ***40*** Minutes

INGREDIENTS

- **1 lb. tenderloins**
- **2 oz. rice noodle**
- **1 carrot**
- **1 celery stalk**
- **1 cucumber**
- **¼ capsicum**
- **1 tablespoon peanuts**

DRESSING

- **1 onion**
- **1 garlic clove**
- **½ cup soy sauce**
- **½ cup rice vinegar**
- **1 tsp sugar**
- **1 tsp sesame oil**

DIRECTIONS

1. **Place all dressing ingredients in a jar and mix well**
2. **In a bowl place all salad ingredients and mix well**
3. **Pour dressing over salad and serve**

SHREDDED SWEET POTATO HASH BROWNS

Serves:	2	
Prep Time:	*10*	minutes
Cook Time:	*30*	minutes
Total Time:	*40*	minutes

INGREDIENTS

- 7 oz. sweet potatoes
- 3 tablespoons butter
- 1 tablespoon dried sage
- 1/8 tablespoon black pepper
- 1/8 tablespoon salt

DIRECTIONS

1. **Shred the potatoes and place them in a strainer.**
2. **Use a rubber spatula and press the excess water.**
3. **Place the potatoes on a paper towel and pat as dry as possible.**
4. **Put the potatoes in a bowl and add sage, salt and pepper.**
5. **Place the butter in a skillet over high heat.**
6. **When the butter is melted add the potatoes.**
7. **Toss well for 5 minutes and gather them together into two piles.**
8. **Cook the potatoes slowly.**
9. **Cook on each side for 3 minutes.**

SPAGHETTI WITH MEATBALLS

Serves: 2

Prep Time: ***10*** minutes

Cook Time: ***35*** minutes

Total Time: ***45*** minutes

INGREDIENTS

- 4 quarts' water
- 5 meatballs
- ½ tomato sauce
- ½ ounces Parmigiano-Reggiano
- 2 ounces' spaghetti noodles

DIRECTIONS

1. **In a large pot add water to high heat**
2. **Add spaghetti noodles**
3. **Add the meatballs and tomato sauce in a medium sauce pan while the pasta is cooking**
4. **Remove the noodles and allow them to drain**
5. **Place the noodles in the sauce with the meatballs**

HOMEMADE CHICKEN NUGGETS

Serves: *4*

Prep Time: *10* Minutes

Cook Time: *30* Minutes

Total Time: *40* Minutes

INGREDIENTS

- 1 lbs. chicken breast
- 2 small eggs
- ¼ tsp garlic powder
- ¼ tsp salt
- ¼ cup breadcrumbs
- 1 ½ cups cauliflower

DIRECTIONS

1. **Preheat oven to 325 F and place a baking tray in**
2. **In a bowl mix garlic powder, salt and egg and whisk together**
3. **In another bowl mix cauliflower and breadcrumbs, dip the chicken into the mixture**
4. **Bake for 20-25 minutes on each side**

GRILLED VEGETABLES

Serves: *4*

Prep Time: *10* Minutes

Cook Time: *10* Minutes

Total Time: *20* Minutes

INGREDIENTS

- 1 tablespoon olive oil
- ¼ tsp salt
- 2 bell peppers
- 1 bunch asparagus
- 2 small zucchinis
- 1 tablespoon rice vinegar
- 1 tablespoon oregano
- 1 eggplant

DIRECTIONS

1. **In a bowl whisk salt, oregano, vinegar and olive oil**
2. **Place the vegetables into a bowl**
3. **Place vegetables on a grill**
4. **Cook eggplant and zucchini pieces for 5-6 minutes per side**
5. **Toss asparagus and cool for 4-5 minutes**
6. **Transfer to a plate and serve when ready**

PORK KEBABS

Serves: *8*

Prep Time: *10* Minutes

Cook Time: *15* Minutes

Total Time: *25* Minutes

INGREDIENTS

- **½ cup fresh basil**
- **22 red globe grapes**
- **¼ Tsp allspice**
- **1 lb. pork loin chop**
- **1 tsp cumin**
- **¼ tsp cardamom**
- **¼ tsp salt**
- **2 tsp fenugreek seeds**
- **¼ black pepper**

DIRECTIONS

1. **In a bowl mix cumin, cardamom, salt, pepper, fenugreek and set aside**
2. **Cut the pork and sprinkle the mixture onto the pork cubes and stir until well coated**
3. **For each kebab slide a cube of pork into the skewer and alternate with basil wrapped grapes**

4. **Preheat the grill and cook for 10-15 minutes**

TUNA PASTA SALAD

Serves: *4*

Prep Time: *10* Minutes

Cook Time: *30* Minutes

Total Time: *40* Minutes

INGREDIENTS

- **3 cups bow tie pasta**
- **1 cup cherry tomatoes**
- **1 tablespoon olive oil**
- **2 tablespoons wine vinegar**
- **1 tsp mustard**
- **¼ cup parsley**
- **1 tin tuna**

DIRECTIONS

1. **Combine all ingredients together and mix well**
2. **Serve when ready**

ROASTED CHICKPEAS

Serves: *4*

Prep Time: *10* Minutes

Cook Time: *30* Minutes

Total Time: *40* Minutes

INGREDIENTS

- 2 cans chickpeas
- 1 tsp olive oil
- 1 tsp salt
- 1 tsp pepper
- 1 tsp thyme
- 1 tsp rosemary

DIRECTIONS

1. Preheat oven to 350 F
2. Line an oven tray with baking paper, toss chickpeas in salt, pepper and oil
3. Pour mixture over baking paper and roast for 20-25 minutes
4. Remove and serve

GRAIN FREE FAJITAS

Serves: *3*

Prep Time: *10* Minutes

Cook Time: *10* Minutes

Total Time: *20* Minutes

INGREDIENTS

- **1 tablespoon avocado oil**
- **3 carrots**
- **3 large nori sheets**
- **1 tomato**
- **1 tablespoon fresh cilantro**
- **1 red pepper**
- **1 green bell pepper**
- **1 while onion**
- **1 jalapeno**

DIRECTIONS

1. **In a skillet sauce avocado oil, onion, jalapeno, white onion, salt and pepper for 6-7 minutes**
2. **Remove from heat and place mixture in a bowl**
3. **Sauté carrots with pepper and salt for 5-6 minutes**
4. **Combine coconut milk with curry powder and combine with red onion, sea s alt and pepper**

5. **Lay the nori sheets and top with pepper mixture and carrots and drizzle with coconut milk**

FISH TACOS

Serves: ***4***

Prep Time: ***10*** Minutes

Cook Time: ***30*** Minutes

Total Time: ***40*** Minutes

INGREDIENTS

- **8 fish fingers**
- **¼ cabbage**
- **tacos**
- **guacamole**
- **2 avocados**
- **salt**
- **coriander**
- **juice of 1 lime**

Salsa

- **2 cherry tomatoes**
- **½ onion**
- **1 tablespoon vinegar**
- **8 jalapeno slices**
- **juice 1 lime**
- **salt**

Spicy mayo

- **½ cup mayo**

- 1 tablespoon paprika
- ½ cup ketchup
- juice 1 lime

DIRECTIONS

1. For salsa add all the ingredients into a blender and blend until smooth, place into a bowl and set aside
2. Mash avocado with salt, lime juice and mix with coriander
3. Mix your spicy mayo in a bowl, heat your tacos and pour the mixture on the tacos
4. Serve when ready

AVOCADO SANDWICH

Serves: *1*

Prep Time: *10* Minutes

Cook Time: *10* Minutes

Total Time: *20* Minutes

INGREDIENTS

- 1 avocado
- juice of 1 lemon pinch of salt
- coriander
- 6 rashers of bacon
- 4 slices bread
- 2 eggs
- ¼ tablespoon hot sauce

DIRECTIONS

1. In a pan add bacon and cook over medium heat
2. In a bowl mix lemon juice, salt, avocado and coriander
3. Toss your bread in the pan and crack an egg into the bread (make a hole before)
4. Add the avocado mixture over the bread and top with bacon

GREEN PESTO PASTA

Serves: 2

Prep Time: 5 Minutes

Cook Time: *15* Minutes

Total Time: *20* Minutes

INGREDIENTS

- 4 oz. spaghetti
- 2 cups basil leaves
- 2 garlic cloves
- ¼ cup olive oil
- 2 tablespoons parmesan cheese
- ½ tsp black pepper

DIRECTIONS

1. Bring water to a boil and add pasta
2. In a blend add parmesan cheese, basil leaves, garlic and blend
3. Add olive oil, pepper and blend again
4. Pour pesto onto pasta and serve when ready

CAULIFLOWER STEAKS WITH LEMON SAUCE

Serves: *4*

Prep Time: *10* Minutes

Cook Time: *10* Minutes

Total Time: *20* Minutes

INGREDIENTS

- **1 head cauliflower**
- **2 tablespoons olive oil**
- **2 tsp paprika**

LEMON SAUCE

- **1 cup parsley leaves**
- **¼ cup mint leaves**
- **1 garlic clove**
- **¼ cup olive oil**
- **¼ cup green onion**
- **Juice of 1 lemon**

DIRECTIONS

1. **In a blender add all ingredients for the lemon sauce and blend until smooth**
2. **For the cauliflower steak, cut cauliflower into thick slices and rub with olive oil**

3. Sprinkle with spices and place the cauliflower in a skillet
4. Cook for 4-5 minutes per side
5. When ready remove and serve with lemon sauce

KUNG PAO CAULIFLOWER

Serves: *4*

Prep Time: *10* Minutes

Cook Time: *30* Minutes

Total Time: *40* Minutes

INGREDIENTS

- **2 tablespoons olive oil**
- **salt**
- **2 scallions**
- **¼ cup cilantro**
- **1 head cauliflower**
- **1 tablespoon sesame seeds**

SAUCE

- **1 tablespoon rice wine vinegar**
- **1 tablespoon ginger**
- **1 tsp olive oil**
- **1 tablespoon soy sauce**
- **1 tablespoon hoisin sauce**

DIRECTIONS

1. **In a bowl combine all sauce ingredients together and mix well**
2. **For the cauliflower heat the olive oil in a skillet and add the cauliflower**

3. Add salt, sesame seeds and cook for 4-5 minutes
4. When ready remove from heat, add cilantro and stir to combine
5. Serve with sauce

RICE, KALE AND AVOCADO BOWL

Serves: 2

Prep Time: *10* Minutes

Cook Time: *20* Minutes

Total Time: *30* Minutes

INGREDIENTS

- **1 cup rice**
- **1 garlic clove**
- **1 tablespoon rice vinegar**
- **2 cups vegetable broth**
- **pinch of salt**
- **pinch of pepper**
- **2 tablespoons**
- **1 bunch kale**
- **1 bunch kale**
- **1 avocado**

DIRECTIONS

1. **In a pot stir in broth, rice and garlic**
2. **Bring to a simmer for and cook until liquid is evaporated**
3. **When ready toss rice with salt, pepper and vinegar**
4. **In another books toss kale with olive oil**

5. **Add kale and avocado slices to the rice**
6. **Serve when ready**

CHICKEN MEATBALLS AND CAULIFLOWER RICE

Serves: ***4***

Prep Time: ***10*** Minutes

Cook Time: ***30*** Minutes

Total Time: ***40*** Minutes

INGREDIENTS

- **¼ cup red onion**
- **1 lb. ground chicken**
- **1 tablespoon mustard**
- **¼ tsp black pepper**
- **1 tablespoon olive oil**
- **1 garlic clove**
- **¼ cup parsley**
- **pinch of salt**

SAUCE

- **1 cup parsley**
- **1 can coconut milk**
- **2 scallions**
- **zest of 1 lemon**
- **1 cup ready-made cauliflower rice**

DIRECTIONS

1. In a skillet heat olive oil and sauté onion and garlic for 3-4 minutes
2. Remove sautéed onion and garlic to a bowl
3. Stir in parsley, mustard, chicken, seasoning and mix well
4. Form balls from the mixture and place on a baking sheet
5. Bake at 400 F for 20 minutes
6. When ready remove from the oven and set aside
7. In a blender add all ingredients for the sauce and blend
8. Top the meatballs with sauce and cauliflower rice and serve

PINEAPPLE CHICKEN AND LETTUCE WRAPS

Serves: 2

Prep Time: *10* Minutes

Cook Time: *20* Minutes

Total Time: *30* Minutes

INGREDIENTS

- **2 cups cooked chicken**
- **1 tablespoon olive oil**
- **¼ tsp paprika**
- **1 tablespoon lime juice**
- **¼ tsp garlic powder**
- **¼ tsp salt**
- **1 cup pineapple cubes**
- **8 lettuce wraps**

DIRECTIONS

1. **In a bowl combine garlic powder, lime juice, paprika, olive oil and lime juice**
2. **In your lettuce wraps add pineapple cubes, chicken and top with lime mixture**
3. **Serve when ready**

ROASTED SALMON WITH POTATOES

Serves: *4*
Prep Time: *10* Minutes

Cook Time: *35* Minutes

Total Time: *45* Minutes

INGREDIENTS

- 1 lb. potatoes
- 1 tsp lemon juice
- 4 salmon fillets
- ¼ tsp paprika
- 2 tablespoons olive oil

DIRECTIONS

1. **Bake the potatoes at 375 F for 20-25 minutes**
2. **Rub the salmon fillets with paprika and olive oil**
3. **Bake the fish until golden brown**
4. **When ready from the oven and serve with baked potatoes and lemon juice**

GUT ENERGY BOOSTING BOWL

Serves: *1*

Prep Time: *5* Minutes

Cook Time: *5* Minutes

Total Time: *10* Minutes

INGREDIENTS

- **2 cups kale**
- **1 tablespoon olive oil**
- **1 avocado**
- **¼ cup carrot**
- **½ cup beans**
- **¼ cup cabbage**
- **1 cup baked potatoes**

DIRECTIONS

1. **In a bowl add all ingredients together**
2. **Drizzle olive oil and salt and mix well**
3. **Serve when ready**

BALED EGGS WITH ZOODLES

Serves: *2*

Prep Time: *5* Minutes

Cook Time: *10* Minutes

Total Time: *15* Minutes

INGREDIENTS

- 2 zucchinis
- pinch of salt
- 2 avocados
- 2 tablespoons olive oil
- 2 eggs
- 1 tablespoon olive oil

DIRECTIONS

1. In a bowl toss the zucchini noodles with olive oil
2. Season and transfer to a baking sheet
3. Crack an egg over each portion
4. Bake for 8-10 minutes at 375 F
5. When ready remove from the oven and serve with avocado slices

CHICKEN WITH BAKED VEGGIES

Serves: ***4***

Prep Time: ***10*** Minutes

Cook Time: ***30*** Minutes

Total Time: ***40*** Minutes

INGREDIENTS

- **1 tablespoon olive oil**
- **1 tablespoon honey**
- **2 red bell peppers**
- **2 carrots**
- **¼ cup parsley**
- **1 lb. chicken breast**
- **2 onions**

DIRECTIONS

1. **Place the chicken onto a baking sheet**
2. **Add the rest of the ingredients to the chicken breast**
3. **Drizzle olive oil over chicken and veggies**
4. **Bake at 375 F for 25-30 minutes or until the vegetables are tender**
5. **When ready remove from the oven and serve**

VEGGIE STIR-FRY

Serves: **2**

Prep Time: ***10*** Minutes

Cook Time: ***20*** Minutes

Total Time: ***30*** Minutes

INGREDIENTS

- 1 tablespoon cornstarch
- 1 garlic clove
- ¼ cup olive oil
- ¼ head broccoli
- ¼ cup show peas
- ½ cup carrots
- ¼ cup green beans
- 1 tablespoon soy sauce
- ½ cup onion

DIRECTIONS

1. In a bowl combine garlic, olive oil, cornstarch and mix well
2. Add the rest of the ingredients and toss to coat
3. In a skillet cook vegetables mixture until tender
4. When ready transfer to a plate garnish with ginger and serve

WALDORF SALAD

Serves: 2

Prep Time: 5 Minutes

Cook Time: 5 Minutes

Total Time: *10* Minutes

INGREDIENTS

- **1 tablespoon mayonnaise**
- **1 tablespoon lemon juice**
- **1 apple**
- **1 cup red grapes**
- **½ cup cranberries**
- **½ cup walnuts**
- **12 cup celery**
- **6 lettuce leaves**

DIRECTIONS

1. **Combine all ingredients together and mix well**
2. **Serve with dressing**

CRANBERRY SALAD

Serves: 2

Prep Time: *5* Minutes

Cook Time: *5* Minutes

Total Time: ***10*** Minutes

INGREDIENTS

- **1 can unsweetened pineapple**
- **1 package cherry gelatin**
- **1 tablespoon lemon juice**
- **½ cup artificial sweetener**
- **1 cup cranberries**
- **1 orange**
- **1 cup celery**
- **½ cup pecans**

DIRECTIONS

1. **Combine all ingredients together and mix well**
2. **Serve with dressing**

ARUGULA SALAD

Serves: *1*

Prep Time: *5* Minutes

Cook Time: *5* Minutes

Total Time: ***10*** Minutes

INGREDIENTS

- **2 cups arugula leaves**
- **¼ cup cranberries**
- **¼ cup honey**
- **¼ cup pecans**
- **1 cup salad dressing**

DIRECTIONS

1. **Combine all ingredients together and mix well**
2. **Serve with dressing**

MANDARIN SALAD

Serves: 2

Prep Time: *10* Minutes

Cook Time: *20* Minutes

Total Time: *30* Minutes

INGREDIENTS

- 2 tsp maple syrup
- 3 tbs oil
- 3 mandarins
- 1 avocado
- 150 g walnuts
- 250 g kale
- 150 g spinach
- 1 lemon
- 150 g Brussels sprouts
- ½ red onion

DIRECTIONS

1. Preheat the oven to 400F
2. Dice the sprouts, red onion, kale and avocado
3. Cut the mandarins
4. Pulse the walnuts just a little using a food processor
5. Mix the walnuts with lemon zest
6. Mix together the maple syrup, oil and lemon juice

7. **Add the walnuts to the vegetables, pour the dressing over and serve**

BEAN FAJITAS

Serves: **2**

Prep Time: ***5*** Minutes

Cook Time: ***10*** Minutes

Total Time: ***15*** Minutes

INGREDIENTS

- **1 kidney beans can**
- **Tortillas**
- **3 tsp cumin**
- **2 tsp garlic powder**
- **5 mushrooms**
- **2 red peppers**
- **2 yellow peppers**
- **1 onion**

DIRECTIONS

1. **Cook the peppers and the onion until caramelized**
2. **Add the mushrooms, garlic powder and cumin**
3. **Add the kidney beans after a few minutes when the mushrooms turn brown**
4. **Cook until soft**
5. **Heat the tortillas**
6. **Fill them with the vegetable mixture and serve**

TOFU SALAD

Serves: *1*

Prep Time: *5* Minutes

Cook Time: *5* Minutes

Total Time: *10* Minutes

INGREDIENTS

- **1 pack tofu**
- **1 cup chopped vegetables (carrots, cucumber)**

DRESSING

- **1 tablespoon sesame oil**
- **1 tablespoon mustard**
- **1 tablespoon brown rice vinegar**
- **1 tablespoon soya sauce**

DIRECTIONS

1. **Combine all ingredients together and mix well**
2. **Add salad dressing, toss well and serve**

PAD THAI SALAD

Serves: *1*

Prep Time: *5* Minutes

Cook Time: *5* Minutes

Total Time: ***10*** Minutes

INGREDIENTS

- ¼ lb. rice noodles
- 1 red pepper
- 1 onion
- 4 stalks coriander
- ¼ package silken tofu
- 1 oz. roasted peanuts
- Salad dressing

DIRECTIONS

1. **Combine all ingredients together and mix well**
2. **Add salad dressing, toss well and serve**

BEEF STEW

Serves: **4**

Prep Time: ***15*** Minutes

Cook Time: ***45*** Minutes

Total Time: ***60*** Minutes

INGREDIENTS

- **2 lb. beef**
- **1 tsp salt**
- **4 tablespoons olive oil**
- **2 red onions**
- **2 cloves garlic**
- **1 cup white wine**
- **2 cups beef broth**
- **1 cup water**
- **3-4 bay leaves**
- **¼ tsp thyme**
- **1 lb. potatoes**

DIRECTIONS

1. **Chop all ingredients in big chunks**
2. **In a large pot heat olive oil and add ingredients one by one**

3. **Cook for 5-6 or until slightly brown**
4. **Add remaining ingredients and cook until tender, 35-45 minutes**
5. **Season while stirring on low heat**
6. **When ready remove from heat and serve**

IRISH STEW

Serves: *4*

Prep Time: *15* Minutes

Cook Time: *45* Minutes

Total Time: *60* Minutes

INGREDIENTS

- **4-5 slices bacon**
- **2 lb. beef**
- **¼ cup flour**
- **½ tsp black pepper**
- **4 carrots**
- **½ cup beef broth**

DIRECTIONS

1. **Chop all ingredients in big chunks**
2. **In a large pot heat olive oil and add ingredients one by one**
3. **Cook for 5-6 or until slightly brown**
4. **Add remaining ingredients and cook until tender, 35-45 minutes**
5. **Season while stirring on low heat**
6. **When ready remove from heat and serve**

CASSEROLE RECIPES

CHICKEN CASSEROLE

Serves: *4*

Prep Time: *10* Minutes

Cook Time: *15* Minutes

Total Time: *25* Minutes

INGREDIENTS

- **1 tablespoon olive oil**
- **1 lb. chicken breast**
- **1 red onion**
- **2 cloves garlic**
- **1 tsp paprika**
- **4 cups cooked rice**
- **¼ cup cranberries**
- **1 lb. brussels sprouts**
- **1 potato**

DIRECTIONS

1. **Sauté the veggies and set aside**
2. **Preheat the oven to 425 F**
3. **Transfer the sautéed veggies to a baking dish, add remaining ingredients to the baking dish**

4. **Mix well, add seasoning and place the dish in the oven**
5. **Bake for 12-15 minutes or until slightly brown**
6. **When ready remove from the oven and serve**

RICE CASSEROLE

Serves: *4*
Prep Time: *10* Minutes

Cook Time: *15* Minutes

Total Time: *25* Minutes

INGREDIENTS

- 2 cups cooked rice
- 1 red onion
- ¼ cup olive oil
- 1 can mushroom soup
- 2 lb. chicken thighs
- 2 tablespoons butter
- 1 clove garlic
- 1 tablespoon parsley

DIRECTIONS

1. **Sauté the veggies and set aside**
2. **Preheat the oven to 425 F**
3. **Transfer the sautéed veggies to a baking dish, add remaining ingredients to the baking dish**
4. **Mix well, add seasoning and place the dish in the oven**
5. **Bake for 12-15 minutes or until slightly brown**
6. **When ready remove from the oven and serve**

MUSHROOM PIZZA

Serves: 2

Prep Time: *10* Minutes

Cook Time: *30* Minutes

Total Time: *40* Minutes

INGREDIENTS

- 2 button mushrooms
- ½ red onion
- 1 lemon juiced
- 1 tablespoon parsley
- ½ cup ground flax seeds
- 2 tablespoons olive oil
- 1 cup almonds whole
- 1 cup cashews whole
- 1 carrot

DIRECTIONS

1. Preheat oven to 375 F and place a baking sheet
2. In food processor place all the ingredients and blend for 8-10 minutes

3. **Pour the mixture on the baking sheet and bake for 15-20 minutes until golden**
4. **Remove from the oven and serve**

CASSEROLE PIZZA

Serves: *6-8*

Prep Time: ***10*** Minutes

Cook Time: *15* Minutes

Total Time: 25 Minutes

INGREDIENTS

- 1 pizza crust
- ½ cup tomato sauce
- ¼ black pepper
- 1 cup zucchini slices
- 1 cup mozzarella cheese
- 1 cup olives

DIRECTIONS

1. **Spread tomato sauce on the pizza crust**
2. **Place all the toppings on the pizza crust**
3. **Bake the pizza at 425 F for 12-15 minutes**
4. **When ready remove pizza from the oven and serve**

SECOND COOKBOOK

FRENCH TOAST

Serves: 2

Prep Time: 5 minutes

Cook Time: 5 minutes

Total Time: **10** minutes

INGREDIENTS

- **1 ½ tsp cinnamon**
- **4 slices bread**
- **2 tsp vanilla**
- **4 eggs**
- **3 tbs milk**

DIRECTIONS

1. **Whisk together the eggs, milk, vanilla and cinnamon in a bowl**
2. **Soak the bread into the mixture**
3. **Heat a greased pan**
4. **Cook the soaked bread for about 2 minutes per side until golden**
5. **Serve immediately**

BREAKFAST QUINOA

Serves: *4*

Prep Time: *10* Minutes

Cook Time: *15* Minutes

Total Time: *25* Minutes

INGREDIENTS

- **1 cup quinoa**
- **2 tbs almonds**
- **3 tbs coconut**
- **1/3 tsp cinnamon**
- **1 cup strawberries**
- **2 cups milk**
- **3 tbs maple syrup**

DIRECTIONS

1. **Place the quinoa and the milk in a pot and bring to a boil**
2. **Reduce the heat and simmer for at least 10 minutes**
3. **Stir in 2 extra tbs of milk, maple syrup and cinnamon**
4. **Divide into bowls and top with strawberries, coconut and almonds**

CHEESE SANDWICH

Serves: *1*

Prep Time: *5* Minutes

Cook Time: *5* Minutes

Total Time: *10* Minutes

INGREDIENTS

- **4 slices tomato**
- **1 oz cheese**
- **2 tbs mayonnaise**
- **1 slice bread**
- **1 can sardines**
- **¼ tsp turmeric**
- **A pinch salt**
- **A pinch black pepper**

DIRECTIONS

1. **Mix the sardines, mayonnaise, turmeric and salt**
2. **Toast the bread**
3. **Spread the mixture over the bread**
4. **Top with tomato slices and then with the cheese slices**
5. **Broil in the preheated oven for 2 minutes**
6. **Serve topped with black pepper**

MORNING POT

Serves: 2

Prep Time: 5 Minutes

Cook Time: 5 Minutes

Total Time: *10* Minutes

INGREDIENTS

- 2 cups coconut milk
- Raspberries
- 1 banana
- ½ cup rolled oats
- Handful spinach leaves
- 1/3 cup chia seeds
- ½ mango
- 1 pear

DIRECTIONS

1. Place the banana, spinach and coconut milk in a food processor and pulse until smooth
2. Stir in the chia seeds and the oats, mixing well
3. Refrigerate covered overnight
4. Peel and dice the mango
5. Top the oats with mango, pear and raspberries
6. Serve when ready

BREAKFAST ROLL-UPS

Serves: 2

Prep Time: 5 Minutes

Cook Time: 5 Minutes

Total Time: *10* Minutes

INGREDIENTS

- **1/3 cup black beans**
- **3 tbs salsa**
- **1 scallion**
- **2 tbs cilantro**
- **2 eggs**
- **1 tortilla**
- **½ avocado**
- **1 tomato**
- **1/3 cup shredded cheese**

DIRECTIONS

1. **Cook the salsa, black beans, cilantro and scallions for about 2 minutes**
2. **Add in the eggs and cook until set**
3. **Heat the tortilla**
4. **Spoon the cooked mixture onto the tortilla, then top with diced avocado, tomato and cheese**

5. **Roll-up the tortilla and cut in half**
6. **Serve immediately**

BANANA BREAD

Serves: *12*

Prep Time: *10* Minutes

Cook Time: *50* Minutes

Total Time: *60* Minutes

INGREDIENTS

- **2 bananas**
- **2 eggs**
- **3 tsp vanilla**
- **1 cup flour**
- **1 tsp cinnamon**
- **½ tsp nutmeg**
- **1 cup grape juice**
- **1 tsp baking soda**
- **1/3 cup walnuts**
- **¼ cup oil**
- **2 tbs baking powder**
- **1/3 cup oat bran**
- **1/3 cup oats**

DIRECTIONS

1. **Mix the banana, oil, eggs, vanilla and eggs in a blender and pulse until smooth**

2. Mix the flaxseed, oats, flour, nutmeg, cinnamon, baking soda and baking powder in a separate bowl and stir well
3. Stir in the banana mixture into the flour mixture, mixing gently
4. Fold in the walnuts
5. Spoon the batter into a greased pan
6. Cook in the preheated oven for 50 minutes at 350F
7. Allow to cool, then serve

BLUEBERRY PANCAKES

Serves: *4*

Prep Time: *10* Minutes

Cook Time: *10* Minutes

Total Time: *20* Minutes

INGREDIENTS

- 2 cup blueberries
- 2 tsp baking powder
- 1 ½ cup flour
- 2 tsp baking soda
- 2 eggs
- 1/3 cup oil
- 1/3 cup grape juice
- 1/3 tsp vanilla
- 1/3 cup oats
- 1 ½ cups buttermilk

DIRECTIONS

1. Mix together the flour, baking powder and baking soda and the oats
2. Whisk the eggs with ¼ cup oil, grape juice and vanilla in a separate bowl
3. Pour the buttermilk and the egg mixture over the dry ingredients

4. **Stir to combine, then fold in the blueberries**
5. **Cook the pancakes in 1 tbs of hot oil**
6. **Cook on both sides until golden brown**
7. **Serve topped with maple syrup**

NUTS AND DATES BARS

Serves: *8*

Prep Time: ***10*** Minutes

Cook Time: ***20*** Minutes

Total Time: ***30*** Minutes

INGREDIENTS

- **4 oz butter**
- **1 oz sesame seeds**
- **1 oz flaxseeds**
- **2 oz nuts**
- **3 oz rolled oats**
- **1 egg**
- **3 oz**
- **4 oz dates**
- **3 tbs syrup**

DIRECTIONS

1. **Mix the butter and the syrup together**
2. **Beat the eggs and mix with the almonds**
3. **Stir in the egg mixture into the butter mixture**
4. **Mix in the remaining ingredients**
5. **Pour into a greased baking tin and bake for at least 20 minutes**

APPLE PORRIDGE

Serves: **2**

Prep Time: *5* Minutes

Cook Time: ***10*** Minutes

Total Time: *15* Minutes

INGREDIENTS

- **Grated apple**
- **1 tsp flaxseed**
- **Handful sultanas**
- **1 ½ tsp maca**
- **Apple puree**
- **Nuts**
- **Honey**
- **Handful cranberries**
- **1 banana**
- **1 dollop yogurt**
- **Blueberries**
- **Raspberries**

DIRECTIONS

1. **Prepare the porridge as you desire**
2. **Stir in the remaining ingredients**
3. **Cook over gentle heat until thick**

MORNING GRANOLA

Serves: 2
Prep Time: *10* Minutes

Cook Time: *20* Minutes

Total Time: *30* Minutes

INGREDIENTS

- **1/3 cup sunflower, pumpkin, sesame and chia seeds**
- **1 cup pecan nuts**
- **2 cups rolled oats**
- **1/3 cup cranberries**
- **1/3 cup almonds**
- **1/3 cup coconut oil**
- **1/3 cup peanut butter**
- **1/3 cup water**
- **½ cup honey**

DIRECTIONS

1. **Mix the dry ingredients together**
2. **Mix the coconut oil, honey, water and peanut butter together in a bowl**
3. **Mix in the wet ingredients into the dry ingredients until combined**
4. **Pour the mixture into a lined baking sheet**

5. **Bake in the preheated oven at 350F for at least 15 minutes**
6. **Allow to cool, then serve**

BLUEBERRY FRENCH TOAST

Serves: *6*

Prep Time: *10* Minutes

Cook Time: *50* Minutes

Total Time: *60* Minutes

INGREDIENTS

- **1 cup blueberries**
- **4 eggs**
- **1 cup coconut milk**
- **¼ cup honey**
- **1 tsp ground cinnamon**
- **1 tablespoon vanilla extract**
- **1 zucchini slice "bread"**

DIRECTIONS

1. **In a baking dish add zucchini "bread" cubes and blueberries**
2. **In a bowl mix honey, coconut milk, eggs, cinnamon and vanilla extract**
3. **Pour egg mixture over bread and bake at 325 F for 45 minutes**

PUMPKIN MUFFINS

Serves: *8*

Prep Time: *10* Minutes

Cook Time: *30* Minutes

Total Time: *40* Minutes

INGREDIENTS

- 5 eggs
- ½ cup pumpkin puree
- ½ tsp baking soda
- ½ cup almond flour
- ¼ tsp salt

TOPPING

- 1 tablespoon unsweetened coconut flakes
- 1 tablespoon cinnamon

DIRECTIONS

1. In a blender add pumpkin, combine eggs and blend until smooth
2. Add baking soda, coconut flour, baking soda, and blend until smooth
3. Divide batter between 8-10 muffin cups
4. In a blender add topping ingredients and blend until smooth
5. Bake muffins for 25 minutes at 325 F, remove and pour topping over

MORNING YOGURT

Serves: *2*

Prep Time: *10* Minutes

Cook Time: *20* Minutes

Total Time: *30* Minutes

INGREDIENTS

- **1 cup SCD Safe homemade yogurt**
- **1-quart almond milk**

DIRECTIONS

1. **In a pot heat milk**
2. **Place yogurt in mason jar**
3. **Place ½ cup of milk into jar and stir until smooth**
4. **Pour remaining milk into mason jar**
5. **Refrigerate overnight and serve in the morning**

CRANBERRY WALNUT SCONES

Serves: *8*

Prep Time: ***10*** Minutes

Cook Time: ***20*** Minutes

Total Time: ***30*** Minutes

INGREDIENTS

- **2 cups almond flour**
- **½ tsp baking soda**
- **1 tablespoon orange zest**
- **½ cup walnuts chopped**
- **1 egg**
- **2 tablespoons unsweetened coconut flakes**

DIRECTIONS

1. **In a blender add all ingredients and blend until smooth**
2. **Transfer dough into a to the oven and bake at 325 F for 15-16 minutes**

PIZZA MUFFINS

Serves: *8*

Prep Time: *10* Minutes

Cook Time: *30* Minutes

Total Time: *40* Minutes

INGREDIENTS

- **1 cup almond flour**
- **½ tsp salt**
- **½ cup cheddar cheese**
- **½ cup parmesan cheese**
- **½ tsp baking soda**
- **4 eggs**
- **½ cup tomato sauce**

DIRECTIONS

1. **In a blender add all ingredients and blend until smooth**
2. **Line a 12 muffin cups with paper and pour batter into each cup**
3. **Bake at 325 for 25 minutes**
4. **Remove from oven and add sauce on each muffin**

CINNAMON CAKE

Serves: *4*

Prep Time: *10* Minutes

Cook Time: *30* Minutes

Total Time: *40* Minutes

INGREDIENTS

- 2 cups almond flour
- ½ cup honey
- 2 eggs
- ¼ tsp salt
- ½ tsp baking soda
- ¼ cup coconut oil

TOPPING

- ¼ cup coconut oil
- 2 tablespoons cinnamon
- ½ cup almonds

DIRECTIONS

1. **In a blender add all ingredients and blend until smooth**
2. **Spread the batter into baking dish**
3. **In a bowl add the topping ingredients and mix well**
4. **Pour topping over cake batter**

5. **Bake the cake for 30 minutes at 325**

ORANGE SCONES

Serves: ***4***

Prep Time: ***10*** Minutes

Cook Time: ***30*** Minutes

Total Time: ***40*** Minutes

INGREDIENTS

- **2 cups almond flour**
- **½ cup honey**
- **1 egg**
- **¼ tsp salt**
- **1 tablespoon orange zest**
- **¼ tsp baking soda**

DIRECTIONS

1. **In a blender add all the ingredients and blend until smooth**
2. **Chill dough in freezer for 15 minutes**
3. **Transfer to a parchment paper line baking sheet**
4. **Bake at 325 F for 30 minutes**

CREPES

Serves: *4*

Prep Time: *10* Minutes

Cook Time: *30* Minutes

Total Time: *40* Minutes

INGREDIENTS

- 2 tablespoons coconut flour
- 3 eggs
- 1 tablespoon coconut oil
- ½ cup water
- 2 tablespoons coconut oil for cooking

DIRECTIONS

1. **In a blender add all ingredients and blend until smooth**
2. **In a frying pan add coconut oil over medium heat**
3. **Pour batter onto the skillet and cook 1-2 minutes per side**

MINI BAGELS

Serves: *12*

Prep Time: *10* Minutes

Cook Time: *30* Minutes

Total Time: *40* Minutes

INGREDIENTS

- 1 cup almond flour
- 2 tablespoons apple cider (SCD Safe)
- ½ tsp salt
- 5 eggs
- 1 tablespoon coconut flour
- 1 tsp baking soda
- 1 tablespoon onion flakes

DIRECTIONS

1. In a blender add all ingredients and blend until smooth
2. Sprinkle bagels dough with onion flakes
3. Bake at 325 F for 15 minutes, remove and serve

PUMPKING CRANBERRY GRANOLA

Serves: *8*

Prep Time: *10* Minutes

Cook Time: *30* Minutes

Total Time: *40* Minutes

INGREDIENTS

- **1 cup almonds**
- **1 cup macadamia nuts**
- **1 tablespoon cinnamon**
- **½ tsp salt**
- **½ cu dried cranberries**
- **1 cup pumpkin seeds**
- **1 cup roasted pumpkin**
- **2 tablespoons honey**

DIRECTIONS

1. **In a bowl place seeds and nuts, cover with water and soak overnight**
2. **Drain and rinse the seeds and nuts**
3. **In a blender add the nuts and seeds and blend until smooth**
4. **Add in the blender honey, cinnamon, pumpkin puree, salt and blend again**
5. **Spread mixture into 2 baking sheets**

6. **Bake at 150 F for 10 hours or until crispy**

ORANGE BISCUITS

Serves: *6*

Prep Time: ***10*** Minutes

Cook Time: ***30*** Minutes

Total Time: ***40*** Minutes

INGREDIENTS

- ¼ cup coconut flour
- ¼ tsp salt
- ¼ tsp baking soda
- 4 eggs
- 1 tablespoon orange zest
- ½ cup cranberries

DIRECTIONS

1. **In a blender add all the ingredients except cranberries**
2. **Remove mixture from blender and add cranberries**
3. **Bake the mixture for 20 minutes at 325 F**
4. **Remove and cool for 15 minutes before serving**

BAGELS

Serves: *6*

Prep Time: *10* Minutes

Cook Time: *30* Minutes

Total Time: *40* Minutes

INGREDIENTS

- **1 cup almond flour**
- **1 tablespoon coconut flour**
- **1 tsp baking soda**
- **1 tablespoon apple cider (SCD safe)**
- **½ tsp salt**
- **5 eggs**

DIRECTIONS

1. **In a blender add, salt, almond flour, coconut flour, eggs and vinegar, blend until smooth**
2. **Place batter in a plastic bag**
3. **Bake at 325 F for 25 minutes**
4. **Remove and let it cook before serving**

LEMON MUFFINS

Serves: *12*

Prep Time: *10* Minutes

Cook Time: *20* Minutes

Total Time: *30* Minutes

INGREDIENTS

- ½ cup coconut flour
- ½ cup honey
- 1 tablespoon lemon zest
- ½ tsp salt
- ½ tsp baking soda
- 3 eggs

DIRECTIONS

1. **In a blender add all the ingredients and blend until smooth**
2. **Spoon batter into muffin pans**
3. **Bake for 325 F and 10-15 minutes, remove and serve**

BREAKFAST BARS

Serves: ***16***

Prep Time: ***10*** Minutes

Cook Time: ***30*** Minutes

Total Time: ***40*** Minutes

INGREDIENTS

- **1 cup almond flour**
- **½ tsp salt**
- **½ cup coconut oil**
- **1 tablespoon honey**
- **1 tablespoon water**
- **1 tsp vanilla extract**
- **½ cup shredded coconut**
- **½ cup pumpkin seeds**
- **½ cup almonds**
- **½ cup raisins**

DIRECTIONS

1. **In a blender add all ingredients and blend until smooth**
2. **Pour dough into a baking dish**
3. **Bake at 325 F for 20 minutes**
4. **Remove and serve**

MORNING SCONES

Serves: *6*
Prep Time: *10* Minutes

Cook Time: *30* Minutes

Total Time: *40* Minutes

INGREDIENTS

- **½ cup coconut flour**
- **½ cup honey**
- **5 eggs**
- **½ tsp salt**
- **½ tsp baking soda**
- **¼ tsp vanilla extract**

DIRECTIONS

1. **In a blender add all ingredients and blend until smooth**
2. **Scoop batter onto a parchment paper**
3. **Bake at 325F for 15 minutes**
4. **Remove, let it cool and serve**

PUMPKIN MUFFINS

Serves: *8*

Prep Time: ***10*** Minutes

Cook Time: ***20*** Minutes

Total Time: ***30*** Minutes

INGREDIENTS

- ¼ cup coconut flour
- ½ cup roasted pumpkin
- 1 tablespoon cinnamon
- 1 tablespoon ginger
- 4 eggs
- ½ cup honey
- ¼ tsp salt
- ½ tsp baking soda

DIRECTIONS

1. **In a blender add all the ingredients and blend until smooth**
2. **Transfer batter into a paper lined muffin pan**
3. **Bake at 325 F for 20 minutes**
4. **Remove, let it cool and serve**

PALEO PORRIDGE

Serves: 2

Prep Time: *10* Minutes

Cook Time: *30* Minutes

Total Time: *40* Minutes

INGREDIENTS

- 2 tablespoons shredded coconut
- 1 tsp cinnamon
- 1 tablespoon chia seeds
- ½ cup walnuts
- ½ tsp salt
- 1 cup boiling water
- 1 tablespoon pumpkin seeds

DIRECTIONS

1. In a blender add all ingredients and blend until smooth
2. Transfer porridge to a bowl
3. Garnish with raisins, shredded coconut and sunflower seeds
4. Serve when ready

STRAWBERRY TART

Serves: *6-8*

Prep Time: *25* Minutes

Cook Time: *25* Minutes

Total Time: *50* Minutes

INGREDIENTS

- pastry sheets
- ½ lb. mascarpone
- 200 ml double cream
- 2 tablespoons sugar
- 2 tablespoons honey
- 2 tablespoons lemon juice
- 1 lb. strawberries

DIRECTIONS

1. **Preheat oven to 400 F, unfold pastry sheets and place them on a baking sheet**
2. **Toss together all ingredients and mix well**
3. **Spread mixture in a single layer on the pastry sheets**
4. **Before baking, decorate with your desired fruits**
5. **Bake at 400 F for 22-25 minutes or until golden brown**

6. **When ready remove from the oven and serve**

HAZELNUT TART

Serves: *6-8*

Prep Time: 25 Minutes

Cook Time: 25 Minutes

Total Time: *50* Minutes

INGREDIENTS

- pastry sheets
- 3 oz. brown sugar
- ¼ lb. hazelnuts
- 100 ml double cream
- 2 tablespoons syrup
- ¼ lb. dark chocolate
- 2 oz. butter

DIRECTIONS

1. Preheat oven to 400 F, unfold pastry sheets and place them on a baking sheet
2. Toss together all ingredients together and mix well
3. Spread mixture in a single layer on the pastry sheets
4. Before baking decorate with your desired fruits
5. Bake at 400 F for 22-25 minutes or until golden brown
6. When ready remove from the oven and serve

PEACH PECAN PIE

Serves: *8-12*

Prep Time: *15* Minutes

Cook Time: *35* Minutes

Total Time: *50* Minutes

INGREDIENTS

- **4-5 cups peaches**
- **1 tablespoon preserves**
- **1 cup sugar**
- **4 small egg yolks**
- **¼ cup flour**
- **1 tsp vanilla extract**

DIRECTIONS

1. **Line a pie plate or pie form with pastry and cover the edges of the plate depending on your preference**
2. **In a bowl combine all pie ingredients together and mix well**
3. **Pour the mixture over the pastry**
4. **Bake at 400-425 F for 25-30 minutes or until golden brown**
5. **When ready remove from the oven and let it rest for 15 minutes**

OREO PIE

Serves: *8-12*

Prep Time: *15* Minutes

Cook Time: *35* Minutes

Total Time: *50* Minutes

INGREDIENTS

- pastry sheets
- 6-8 oz. chocolate crumb piecrust
- 1 cup half-and-half
- 1 package instant pudding mix
- 10-12 Oreo cookies
- 10 oz. whipped topping

DIRECTIONS

1. Line a pie plate or pie form with pastry and cover the edges of the plate depending on your preference
2. In a bowl combine all pie ingredients together and mix well
3. Pour the mixture over the pastry
4. Bake at 400-425 F for 25-30 minutes or until golden brown
5. When ready remove from the oven and let it rest for 15 minutes

GRAPEFRUIT PIE

Serves: *8-12*

Prep Time: *15* Minutes

Cook Time: *35* Minutes

Total Time: *50* Minutes

INGREDIENTS

- pastry sheets
- 2 cups grapefruit
- 1 cup brown sugar
- ¼ cup flour
- 5-6 egg yolks
- 5 oz. butter

DIRECTIONS

1. **Line a pie plate or pie form with pastry and cover the edges of the plate depending on your preference**
2. **In a bowl combine all pie ingredients together and mix well**
3. **Pour the mixture over the pastry**
4. **Bake at 400-425 F for 25-30 minutes or until golden brown**
5. **When ready remove from the oven and let it rest for 15 minutes**

SMOOTHIE RECIPES

TURMERIC-MANGO SMOOTHIE

Serves: *1*
Prep Time: *5* Minutes

Cook Time: *5* Minutes

Total Time: ***10*** Minutes

INGREDIENTS

- **1 cup Greek yogurt**
- **¼ cup orange juice**
- **1 banana**
- **1 tablespoon turmeric**
- **1 tsp vanilla extract**
- **1 cup ice**

DIRECTIONS

1. **In a blender place all ingredients and blend until smooth**
2. **Pour smoothie in a glass and serve**

AVOCADO-KALE SMOOTHIE

Serves: *1*

Prep Time: 5 Minutes

Cook Time: 5 Minutes

Total Time: *10* Minutes

INGREDIENTS

- 1 cup coconut milk
- 1 tablespoon lemon juice
- 1 bunch kale
- 1 cup spinach
- ¼ avocado
- 1 cup ice

DIRECTIONS

1. **In a blender place all ingredients and blend until smooth**
2. **Pour smoothie in a glass and serve**

BUTTERMILK SMOOTHIE

Serves: *1*

Prep Time: *5* Minutes

Cook Time: *5* Minutes

Total Time: *10* Minutes

INGREDIENTS

- 1 cup ice
- 1 cup strawberries
- 1 cup blueberries
- 1 cup buttermilk
- ½ tsp vanilla extract

DIRECTIONS

1. In a blender place all ingredients and blend until smooth
2. Pour smoothie in a glass and serve

GREEN SMOOTHIE

Serves: *1*

Prep Time: *5* Minutes

Cook Time: *5* Minutes

Total Time: *10* Minutes

INGREDIENTS

- 1 cup berries
- 1 cup baby spinach
- 1 tablespoon orange juice
- ¼ cup coconut water
- ½ cup Greek yogurt

DIRECTIONS

1. **In a blender place all ingredients and blend until smooth**
2. **Pour smoothie in a glass and serve**

FRUIT SMOOTHIE

Serves: *1*

Prep Time: *5* Minutes

Cook Time: *5* Minutes

Total Time: ***10*** Minutes

INGREDIENTS

- 1 mango
- 1 cup vanilla yogurt
- 2 tablespoons honey
- 1 tablespoon lime juice
- 1 banana
- 1 can strawberries
- 1 kiwi

DIRECTIONS

1. **In a blender place all ingredients and blend until smooth**
2. **Pour smoothie in a glass and serve**

MANGO SMOOTHIE

Serves: *1*

Prep Time: *5* Minutes

Cook Time: *5* Minutes

Total Time: *10* Minutes

INGREDIENTS

- 2 cups mango
- 1 cup buttermilk
- 1 tsp vanilla extract
- 1 cup kiwi
- ½ cup coconut milk

DIRECTIONS

1. **In a blender place all ingredients and blend until smooth**
2. **Pour smoothie in a glass and serve**

DREAMSICLE SMOOTHIE

Serves: *1*

Prep Time: *5* Minutes

Cook Time: *5* Minutes

Total Time: ***10*** Minutes

INGREDIENTS

- 1 cup Greek yogurt
- 1 cup ice
- ¼ cup mango
- 1 orange
- 1 pinch cinnamon

DIRECTIONS

1. **In a blender place all ingredients and blend until smooth**
2. **Pour smoothie in a glass and serve**

RICOTTA ICE-CREAM

Serves: *6-8*

Prep Time: *15* Minutes

Cook Time: *15* Minutes

Total Time: *30* Minutes

INGREDIENTS

- 1 cup almonds
- 1-pint vanilla ice cream
- 2 cups ricotta cheese
- 1 cup honey

DIRECTIONS

1. In a saucepan whisk together all ingredients
2. Mix until bubbly
3. Strain into a bowl and cool
4. Whisk in favorite fruits and mix well
5. Cover and refrigerate for 2-3 hours
6. Pour mixture in the ice-cream maker and follow manufacturer instructions
7. Serve when ready

SAFFRON ICE-CREAM

Serves: *6-8*

Prep Time: *15* Minutes

Cook Time: *15* Minutes

Total Time: *30* Minutes

INGREDIENTS

- 4 egg yolks
- 1 cup heavy cream
- 1 cup milk
- ½ cup brown sugar
- 1 tsp saffron
- 1 tsp vanilla extract

DIRECTIONS

1. In a saucepan whisk together all ingredients
2. Mix until bubbly
3. Strain into a bowl and cool
4. Whisk in favorite fruits and mix well
5. Cover and refrigerate for 2-3 hours
6. Pour mixture in the ice-cream maker and follow manufacturer instructions
7. Serve when ready

THANK YOU FOR READING THIS BOOK!

CPSIA information can be obtained
at www.ICGtesting.com
Printed in the USA
BVHW031359220321
603177BV00007B/389